Joseph H. Newton

An Appeal to the Latter-day Saints

Joseph H. Newton

An Appeal to the Latter-day Saints

ISBN/EAN: 9783337337483

Printed in Europe, USA, Canada, Australia, Japan

Cover: Foto ©Lupo / pixelio.de

More available books at **www.hansebooks.com**

AN APPEAL

TO THE

LATTER-DAY SAINTS.

BY

JOSEPH H. NEWTON, WILLIAM RICHARDS,
and WILLIAM STANLEY.

PHILADELPHIA:
PRINTED FOR THE AUTHORS.
1863.

AUTHORS' PREFACE.

We have been induced to send forth this Appeal from considerations of no personal advantage to us, as all will see who give it a careful reading.

In examining our books, which we acknowledge as revelations, we found it was required of all those who believed them to give heed to them, and more particularly as it was there said that the whole church was under condemnation, and would remain so till they returned to the Book of Mormon, and the former commandments which they had received.

In obedience to this command we retired and for many years have devoted ourselves to the continued investigation of these books, and the result of this investigation we here present.

The subject of this Appeal during all this time was far from us; we heard nothing of him for many years, till being moved upon by the Spirit of Holiness, we addressed a letter to the place where we knew he once lived, and found he was still there. The same Spirit that directed us to write to him has required us to send forth this Appeal.

During our long and protracted investigation we

knew not in what point of light the Lord viewed us. Did he acknowledge us in the authority of our former priesthood, or did he not? was an anxious inquiry with us. We did not know, and we dare not venture to act till the case was settled. An event transpired now which put this matter at rest. A man of high standing, and of position and influence in the world, a doctor of learning and talents, came to Joseph H. Newton and sought baptism, and holy administration at his hands, declaring the Lord had sent him to him for this purpose. This event put the great question at rest, as we were sure that the Lord would not have converted a man himself and sent him to us to be administered to, unless he acknowledged us in our priesthood. We stepped forward, as the Spirit required, and thus began again to move in the cause of God.

We will close by saying that to us personally it is of little consequence who receives or who rejects our Appeal. From the knowledge we have obtained of the course the Lord is going to pursue to bring to pass the work of *preparing* to fulfil the covenant to the House of Israel, there are enough of us now to do it, should not one more unite with us. We are induced only to send this to you, because the Lord required us to do so.

JOSEPH H. NEWTON,
WM. RICHARDS,
WM. STANLEY.

OUR APPEAL.

In presenting our appeal to our former brethren, we do it as we feel ourselves authorized, by the revelations vouchsafed to us and them, through the Spirit of Holiness. "To the law and to the testimony," has been the maxim with those who have dealt in sacred matters through all ages, and we follow their example. Having been devoted to the study of the books which we all acknowledge as the basis of our religious faith, to them we direct the attention of all to whom this our appeal may come.

In respect to the relation which the books bear to us, in things pertaining to salvation, we shall refer to them as we find it written therein.

SECTION I.

We will begin with the Book of Doctrine and Covenants, section 1st, paragraph 2d: "For what I the Lord have decreed, in them, shall be fulfilled;" and in the 7th paragraph of the same section we have these impressive words: "Search the commandments, for they are true and faithful, and the prophecies and promises which are in them, shall all be fulfilled." In the 4th section and

7th paragraph, the Spirit speaketh thus: "And now I give unto you a commandment, to beware concerning yourselves, to give diligent heed to the words of eternal life, for you shall live by every word which proceedeth forth from the mouth of God." And in the 8th paragraph of the same section, where the Church was charged with being under condemnation, it is said: "And this condemnation resteth upon the children of Zion, even all; and they shall remain under this condemnation until they repent and remember the new Covenant, even the Book of Mormon, and the former commandments which I have given them." We here take one sentence from the 6th paragraph of the 9th section: "For ye shall do according to that which is written." The following sentence we quote from the 30th section and 1st paragraph: "For God doth not walk in crooked paths; neither doth he turn to the right hand or left; neither doth he vary from that which he has said." A few sentences found in the 37th section and 10th paragraph will give increased evidence to the relation we bear to the written word of the Lord. "Study my word which hath gone forth among the children of men (the Bible); and also study my word which *shall* come forth among the children of men, or that which is now translating."

These requirements were made of Hiram Smith, while the Book of Mormon was yet translating. We refer to them to show the imperious character of the duty imposed on the saints, to study the written word of the Lord.

The following were given to Oliver Cowdery, while he was writing the Book of Mormon, as translated by Joseph

Smith, 43d section, 1st paragraph: "Behold I have manifested unto you, by my Spirit, in many instances, that the things which you have written are true. Wherefore, you know that they are true; and if you know that they are true, behold I give unto you a commandment, that you *rely* upon the things which are *written;* for in them are all things written concerning the foundation of my church, my gospel, and my rock."

As enough has surely been written, as touching the Book of Doctrine and Covenants, on this subject, let us see what the Book of Mormon says with regard to it. In the 4th chapter of the 1st Book of Nephi, where he described what he saw in his great vision, in which the things his father had seen before, were explained to him: when his father had his vision of the mist of darkness and the rod of iron which lead to the tree of life. Nephi was asked in his vision, what the rod of iron meant that his father had seen; he answered, that it was the word of God, and then adds, that whosoever would hearken unto the *word* of God, and would *hold fast* unto it, they would never perish; neither could the temptations and fiery darts of the adversary overpower them unto blindness, to lead them away to destruction.

We cannot conceive of anything more forcible than these words are. The prophet says that by *holding on to the word* of God, you can pass safely through any mist of darkness; it matters not how thick it is, nor how long it lasts, it will guide you safely through. No fiery dart of the adversary can overpower you. No temptation of Satan, so cunningly devised, that it will overcome you;

and no darkness and confusion can blind your mind so as to prevail against you.

In the 3d chapter of the first Book of Nephi, the prophet thus speaks, concerning the Book of Mormon. "It shall make known that the Lamb of God is the Son of the eternal Father, and the Savior of the world, and that all men must come unto him, or they cannot be saved, and they must come according to the *words* which shall be established by the mouth of the Lamb." May we not pause and ask, How can we come to Christ according to the *words* he has established, unless we study that word?

In these teachings of the prophet, the necessity of giving diligent attention to the written revelations of heaven is indispensable for all saints; for these testimonies must be false, or else there is no possibility of persons continuing in the truth by any other means, than that of making themselves acquainted with the wisdom of heaven, as he has caused it to be *written* for our instruction in righteousness.

In the 5th chapter of the first Book of Nephi, the whole case is set forth in clearness and force. In speaking of the leading of the children of Israel in the days of Moses, Nephi says, "And it came to pass that according to his *word*, he did destroy them; and according to his *word*, he did lead them; and according to his *word*, he did do all things for them: and there was not anything done save it were by his *word*."

Put all the above quotations together, and the subject assumes an attitude of importance surpassed by none other; indeed to us it is the all things.

The prophet, when thus speaking of leading the Israelites, the object he had was to enforce upon the minds of his readers the necessity of attending to the *written word;* a something which is everywhere enforced, in the Bible, the Book of Mormon, or that of the Doctrine and Covenants.

While on this subject the words of Christ to the Nephites, at a time when he manifested himself to them, as recorded in the 12th chapter of the Book of the last Nephi, are conclusive. They read thus : " And it shall come to pass that whoso repenteth and is baptized in my name, shall be filled; and if he endure to the end, behold, him will I hold guiltless before my Father, at that day when I shall stand to judge the world. And he that endureth not unto the end, the same is he that is also hewn down and cast into the fire, from whence they can no more return, because of the justice of the Father; and this is the *word* which he hath spoken unto the children of men. And for this cause he fulfilleth the *words* which he hath given, and he lieth not, but fulfilleth all his *words.*"

In order to see the extent of the requirement, hear what Christ said, at another time, to the Nephites. They are recorded in the 10th chapter of the last Nephi. After reiterating what Isaiah had written, he adds: " And now behold, I say unto you that ye ought to search these things. Yea, a commandment I give unto you, that ye search these things diligently; for great are the words of Isaiah. For, surely, he spake as touching all things concerning my people which are of the house of Israel; therefore it must needs be that he must speak also to the Gentiles. And all things that he spake, hath been and shall be, even according to the *words* which he spake. Therefore give heed to my *words;* write the things which I have told you; and according to the time and the will of the Father, they shall go forth unto the Gentiles. And whosoever will hearken unto my *words*, and repenteth, and is baptized, the same shall be saved. *Search* the prophets, for many there be that testify of these things."

It is only necessary to remark here, that no people ever had the Book of Mormon as we have it but ourselves. It was written, at different times, through many generations, and no one people ever had the whole of it till it came to us; so that what is said in it is peculiarly ours.

The quotations noted above are so explicit that none need mistake.

A few reflections upon the purport of the preceding quotations, are all that will be required to enable the reader to see their force.

The study of the Book of Doctrine and Covenants is enforced from the fact that all things therein decreed *shall* be fulfilled, and also that the prophecies and promises in it *shall* be fulfilled. Such being the case, we are commanded to study them, for all things pertaining to the church of Christ shall be according to the *words* recorded in these books; hence the Lord says, " Give *diligent* heed to my *words*, for we are to *live* by every *word* which proceedeth forth from the mouth of God;" but what gives the most absolute force to the duty of studying the written word, is what is declared concerning Zion, where it is said that she is under condemnation, and that she must *remain* under that condemnation until her people return to the Book of Mormon and the former commandments they had received until they did that their *condemnation* was certain, for nothing but that could redeem them from it. Could anything be more impressive than that, under condemnation, and but one way to get from under it,—return to the Book of Mormon and the former commandments? Such is the importance the Lord attached to his written word.

We are therefore required to do according to that which is *written;* for the Lord neither turns to the right hand or left, nor varies from what he *says.* It is enjoined upon us to *rely* on the books, because all things are there written concerning the foundation of the church, the gospel and the rock. Not only are we bound by the law of heaven to study the Books of Mormon and of Doctrine and Covenants, but the prophecy of Isaiah and other prophets, because Isaiah had written of all things pertaining to Israel; and all things concerning Israel should take place according to his *word.*

In doing as the Lord had thus commanded, we have the assurance given us that all the fiery darts of the adversary will be hurled at us in vain. By holding on to the rod of iron, which is the *written* word of God, we are promised a safe passage through every mist of darkness with which Satan may shroud us in; can escape all the snares of the adversary; all the devices and artifices of those who lay in wait to deceive. Yea, can put all the powers of men and devils at defiance, safely reach the tree of life, and fall down and partake of the fruit thereof; but on the contrary, if we do it not, we will fall under condemnation, be bound under chains of darkness, and be cut down and cast into the fire. There is no other way then for us to do, than to study his *word*, rely upon his *word*, hold on to his *word*, and do all things according to his *word*, and triumph in righteousness with him.

SECTION II.

The question now arises, What do these books teach us? We are told, to begin with : that all the prophecies and promises in them shall be fulfilled; and that all things pertaining to Zion shall take place as set forth in the words of these books. Let us see what the prophecies, promises and words are.

The 30th section and 6th paragraph gives us the grand object for which the Book of Mormon and the subsequent revelations were translated and given. Joseph Smith, the translator and revelator, was sorely reproved of the Lord for having transgressed his commandments while translating the plates, and was threatened with being cut off, unless he obeyed more strictly the injunctions laid upon him : the 6th paragraph was said to him, to let him know that though he fell, still that would not prevent the Lord from accomplishing the object for which the plates had been preserved. The Lord, after telling him that he was in danger of being cut off, said, "Nevertheless my work shall go forth, for, inasmuch as the knowledge of a Savior has come into the world, through the Jews, even so shall the knowledge of a Savior come unto my people; and to the Nephites, the Jacobites, and the Josephites, and the Zoramites, through the testimony of their fathers; and this testimony shall come to the Lamanites, and the Lemuelites, and the Ishmaelites, who dwindled in unbelief, because of the iniquity of their fathers, whom the Lord has suffered to destroy their brethren, the Nephites, because of their iniquities and their abominations: and for this very purpose are these plates preserved, which contain these records, that the promises of the Lord might be fulfilled, which he made to his people; and that the Lamanites might come to a knowledge of their fathers, and that they might know the promises of the Lord, and that they may believe the gospel and rely upon the merits of Jesus Christ, and be glorified through faith on his name; and that through their repentance they might be saved: Amen."

It is unnecessary to refer to any other of the declarations to set forth the object of the Book of Mormon and the subsequent revelations. Here it is made known, in language not to be mistaken, that all took place for the redemption of Israel: not only those on this continent but others; for the Spirit says that the knowledge of these things shall come to the *people* of the Lord; and then speaks of the house of Israel on this continent, making a distinction between the *people* spoken of, and the house of Israel on this continent.

While on the subject of gathering Israel, it may be proper, at this place, to refer to the prophecies which make known the fact, that Israel is to be gathered before Christ comes: Book of Doctrine and Covenants, section 13th, paragraph 10th, where the Spirit, after giving directions concerning the management of the temporal matters of the church, says: "Therefore, the residue shall be kept in my store-house, to administer to the poor and needy, as shall be appointed by the high council of the church, and the Bishop and his council, and for the purpose of purchasing lands for the public benefit of the church, and building houses of worship, and building up the New Jerusalem which is hereafter to be revealed, *that my covenant people may be gathered in one, on that day, when I shall come to my temple.* And this I do for the salvation of my people."

The Spirit says, in this quotation, that the covenant people are to be gathered when the Lord comes to his temple.

One more on this subject from the Book of Mormon, 10th chapter of the last Nephi, speaking of the Gentiles. "And they shall assist my people, the remnant of Jacob; and also, as many of the house of Israel as shall come, that they may build a city, which shall be called the New Jerusalem; and then shall they assist my people, that they may be gathered in, who are scattered on the face of the land, in unto the New Jerusalem. And then shall the power of heaven come down among them; and I also will be in the midst."

These prophecies are both to the same import,—that the gathering of Israel is to take place before the coming of the Savior; and that the gathering of the house of Jacob is the way by which his messenger will prepare for his coming.

SECTION III.

After the fact is clearly established, that the work of

the Lord, which commenced by bringing forth the Book of Mormon, was for the purpose of gathering the scattered covenant people, and in so doing, prepare the way for the coming of the Lord, let us see in what relation the prophecies delivered by Joseph Smith, place him and his organization to this great and marvellous work.

In the 20th section and 8th paragraph of the Doctrine and Covenants, we have a prophecy which reads as follows: "Wherefore the land of Zion shall not be obtained but by purchase, or by blood, otherwise there is *none* inheritance for you. And if by purchase, behold you are blessed; and if by blood, as you are forbid to shed blood, lo, your enemies are upon you, and ye shall be scourged from city to city, and from synagogue to synagogue, *and but few will stand to get an inheritance.*"

Who of us do not know, that the driving and scourging here spoken of, has been fulfilled on the head of that people to the uttermost. Surely none. The scourging and driving, however, could be contemplated with a degree of satisfaction, if it were not for what follows, "*and but few will stand to get an inheritance.*" Thus, discouragingly, did Joseph Smith prophesy concerning his organization. If then, *all* the prophecies of this book are to be fulfilled—and if they are not, then the book invalidates itself, for it says they shall—then few of those who composed the organization of Joseph Smith will get an inheritance.

There is written in the 21st section and 7th paragraph another prophecy of Joseph Smith, concerning the church he established, to which we will direct the attention of the reader. It is couched in language to this effect.

"Behold the Lord requireth the heart and a willing mind; and the willing and obedient shall eat the good of the land of Zion in these last days; and the rebellious shall be cut off out of the land of Zion, *and shall be sent away,* and shall not inherit the land."

Let the reader keep in mind that these words were delivered by Joseph Smith in relation to his own fraternity. He said first that they "should be scourged from city to city, and from synagogue to synagogue; and few would stand to get an inheritance;" and in this last quotation, "that they should be cut off out of the land of Zion, and *sent away*, and should not inherit the land."

The first of these prophecies has been fulfilled: and what of the second? Go to Nauvoo, behold the desolation there. Nauvoo is called a toe-stake of Zion. See that great people cut off, driven out, and sent away: and then ask yourself, Is not the second one fulfilled also?

May we not say to those, our former brethren, Read, pause, and reflect. Behold that mighty people, once so great, who "built and inhabited; planted and eat the fruit thereof;" GREAT, so there were none to make them afraid: now far, far away; hundreds of miles stretching their gloomy length between them and any place, the Spirit of revelation, called Zion, or any of her stakes; and can you avoid saying that the solemn prophecy of their founder, quoted above, has been sustained to the very letter?

Joseph Smith did not end his prophesying in relation to them here, but has left others on record, to which we will now refer, in the 104th section and in the 9th and 10th paragraphs. The Spirit, in the 9th paragraph, pronounced the judgment of heaven on the world for their wickedness, and declares that the judgment there threatened should commence on the Lord's house. "And upon my house shall it begin ; and from my house shall it go forth, saith the Lord. First among those among *you*, saith the Lord, who have professed to know my name, and have not known me, and have blasphemed against me in the midst of my house, saith the Lord."

To see the full force of these sayings, it is only necessary to understand that the revelation, from whence we have taken the above testimony, was delivered by Joseph Smith to the twelve of his order, and was said to them, and about them only. They were charged with professing to know the Lord, but did not know him ; and, in consequence of that the Spirit said, in doing so, that they blasphemed against the Lord in his house. Such was the character that Joseph Smith gave to the twelve of his organization.

The only light in which the revelations, concerning them, present their character now, as they are altogether at Utah, is that of a rebellious people ruled by twelve blasphemers; and Joseph Smith gives us a prophecy relating to their fate where they are in their present condition ; for they are where they have been sent, and we read the record the Spirit has kept, and they have left behind them.

They are at this time in the place where the Lord sent them, and he indited a prophecy to be written, telling what awaits them hereafter. It will be found in 98th section and 6th paragraph of the Book of Doctrine and Covenants, and is in words as follow. We will quote the whole paragraph, though it is a long one. "And now, I will show unto you a parable, that you may know my will concerning the redemption of Zion: A certain nobleman had a spot of land, very choice; and he said unto his servants, Go ye into my vineyard, even on this choice piece of land, and plant twelve olive-trees; and set watchmen round about them, and build a tower, that one may overlook the land round about, to be a watchman upon the tower; that mine olive-trees may not be broken down when the enemy shall come to spoil and take unto themselves the fruit of my vineyard. Now the servants of the nobleman went and did as their lord commanded them; and planted the olive-trees, and built a hedge round about, and set watchmen, and began to build a tower. And while they were yet laying the foundation thereof, they began to say among themselves, And what need hath my lord for this tower? And consulted a long time, saying among themselves, What need hath my lord for this tower, seeing this is a time of peace? Might not this money be given to the exchangers? for there is no need of these things! And while they were at variance one with another, they became very slothful, and they hearkened not unto the commandments of their lord, and the enemy came by night, and broke down the hedge, and the servants of the nobleman arose, and were affrighted, and fled; and the enemy destroyed their works, and broke down the olive-trees."

The parabolical prophecy here quoted, cannot be executed only in one place. There never was but the one place where it could take place, nor there never will be but one; and that is at Utah. It is there, and there only, where the twelve got their rule established. There they did do it. It was attempted at Nauvoo; but that being a place where the Lord had placed his saints, he said they should not pollute his land with their abominations, and he cut them off out of Zion, and from all its dominions, and sent them away, to plant their olive-trees elsewhere than on his consecrated land; and after wandering for a long time, they finally reached Salt Lake, and there planted their olive-trees; and the Spirit of revelation which was in their prophet recorded the prophecy, that we are now examining. It portends their entire overthrow. The trees broken down, their works destroyed; the people affrighted and fled away. The concern desolated.

The revelation was written in view of the redemption of Zion. It begins thus: "And now I will show unto you a parable, that you may know my will concerning the redemption of Zion." He then informs us that the order of things set forth in this parable had to transpire before the redemption of Zion. The parable was written twelve years before the order of the twelve was attempted; and such a thought as there being an order of things like that set up, had never entered the head of one individual. But the prophecy was delivered, and the facts have sustained it. The order absolutely has come into existence, and its fate was foretold twelve years before its appearance.

The parable contemplates the people who are described by it, as existing for a length of time in the place where they were, before their destruction came. They had built; placed watchmen; arranged their concerns for life: when, at an unexpected time, they were fallen upon and entirely desolated, and laid waste.

So much for attempting to prevent the order of heaven, by trying to set up the rule of twelve over the Church of the living God.

Solemn reflections suggest themselves to the mind of the sober-thinking, contemplating these awful events. Here ends the organization of Joseph Smith. Gone, gone forever! From the downfall of Utah, it ceases to exist. So says its prophet and founder.

In looking over the history of this people, and their doings and sufferings, what a crowd of forbidding occurrences force themselves on the mind. Joseph Smith gone; the Smith family desolated; the church they established scattered into fragments, and exists no more forever. Why all these things? Their prophet and revelator gives us but one reason. They had fallen under condemnation, from which they could never be delivered only by returning to the Book of Mormon and former commandments which they had received. This they never did, as all know who are acquainted with these books; for, if they had done so, the rule of the twelve would never have existed. Their neglecting these books was their fatal error.

To us who believe in the Book of Mormon, and in the Book of Doctrine and Covenants, the everlasting overthrow of the twelve and the scattering of their people, is as much a fact, in our minds, as if it had now taken place. And how could it be otherwise? The prophecy concerning their being driven and scourged from place to place, has been fulfilled. The prophecy that they should be cut off and sent away from the land of Zion, has also been fulfilled, and the prophecy that they would plant the twelve olive-trees, or organize themselves under the rule of the twelve, is fulfilled to the letter. How then can it be otherwise than that the remaining one, of their overthrow and destruction, will be fulfilled too? From what we have quoted from the Book of Doctrine and Covenants, "that *all* the prophecies and promises in it shall be fulfilled," if this one is not, then the book falsifies itself, and becomes an absurdity, and unworthy of regard.

In those teachings the books have reached an important point. Joseph Smith dead; his father's family desolated; the church he established scattered and gone to be no more forever; and yet Israel not gathered; Zion not redeemed; the way for the coming of the Savior not prepared: yet, the book says that the preservation of the plates, from which the Book of Mormon was translated, was done for the purpose of gathering Israel; and it mattered not what should take place, nothing could prevent the gathering of Israel.

That the parable contemplated the entire abolishment of the society arranged by Joseph Smith, is put beyond doubt, by referring to the 7th paragraph of this 98th section, after setting forth the entire destruction of the order of the twelve. "And the Lord of the vineyard said unto *one* of his servants, Go and gather together the residue of my servants," &c. Now behold the difference: *one* servant called on, not *twelve*. The twelve now gone, and their people with them, and the Lord's calling on *one* servant, shows the contrast between the Lord's manner of working and that of the twelve. He works with *one*, not *twelve*.

Notice, particularly, that the servant here spoken of is working for the Lord after the twelve and their people are gone. If nothing else settles the question, this does, that the twelve and their association had been cut off without gathering Israel; for had they have done that, there would have been no residue for this servant to gather together. There is a confirmation of this in the prophecy of Malachi. The part of the prophecy which contains this confirmation, is transferred into the Book of Mormon, to let us know that it is to be fulfilled now, in this last work of gathering Israel and preparing the way for the coming of the Savior. We quote it as found in the Book of Mormon, the 11th chapter of the last Nephi : " Behold, I will send my messenger, and he shall prepare my way before me, and the Lord whom ye seek shall suddenly come to his temple."

Here we have it certain, that when the way is prepared, the Lord will *suddenly* come to his temple. So if the twelve had done this work, there would be nothing for the servant to do afterwards. Christ would be here, and the work all done. There is a painful thought connected with the work of that servant. He was to gather up the *residue;* not the unfortunate ones, who were broken down, affrighted, fled, and their works destroyed. May we not exclaim : Oh ! our God ! is there not to be one of that unfortunate people to have an inheritance with the saints of the Most High ? But here we leave it.

After the destruction of the twelve, we have the Lord working, but it is always with *one* servant or *one* messenger, and not twelve; *that* order has passed away forever. But now comes the inquiry, Who is this messenger or this servant? We are told that such a one is to work, but we have now to inquire who this messenger or servant is? This brings us to our fourth section.

SECTION IV.

That this servant or messenger is the same person, can admit of no doubt: gathering up the residue was the way to prepare for the coming of Christ. In searching after this person, we will do as we are required to do. "Turn to the Book of Mormon and the former commandments," 8th section and 13th paragraph of Doctrine and Covenants, we read thus: "And now behold I give unto you (O. Cowdery), and also unto my servant Joseph, the keys of this gift, which shall bring to light this ministry." What ministry? Surely the ministry which was to finish the work of bringing to pass the restoration of Israel; for this was the work that was to be done: gather Israel, and through these means prepare the way for the coming of Christ. It is worthy of remark here, that the Spirit did not say, I give to you this ministry, but the keys to bring it to light. Did they bring it to light? In the 11th section and 2d paragraph, the following things on this subject are found. Let us here state a fact, in relation to this revelation. It was written the first time that Joseph Smith and Sidney Rigdon met; they had never seen each other till then. "Behold, verily, verily I say unto my servant Sidney. I have looked upon thee and thy works. I have heard thy prayers, and prepared thee for a greater work. Thou art blessed, for thou shalt do great things. Behold thou wast sent forth even as John, *to prepare the way before me, and before Elijah which should come.*"

Oliver Cowdery and Joseph Smith were told that they had the keys of this gift which should bring to light this ministry; and they say of Sidney Rigdon: "*Thou art the man;*" and who dare say that they falsified? Here the great question is settled. Those to whom it was given to point out this ministry, have pointed to the very man, calling him by name. No dispute can ever exist among those who turn to the Book of Mormon and the former commandments about it. Sidney Rigdon then is the messenger spoken of in Malachi : he is the one who is to gather up the residue, after all others are broken and scattered.

It appears further that he was called to this work before he and Joseph ever saw each other, for the Spirit says: "Thou *wast* sent forth even as John to prepare the way," &c. It does not say, I *will* send thee forth, but thou *wast* sent forth before this time. Here is a great fact disclosed,—that Joseph Smith was never called to gather Israel and prepare the way before Christ, but another man. He (Joseph) had the gift to make known who it was the Lord had chosen for this greatest of all works, but was not the man himself to do it.

To those who are seeking for an hereditary priesthood out of the family of Joseph Smith, we say they may get as many as their fancy may require, but they will never get one that will gather Israel and prepare the way before Christ, for Joseph Smith was never called to this work;

nor never held the priesthood that was appointed for that purpose.

To this end let us call the attention of our readers to the 84th section, 3d paragraph, which gives the following important intelligence: "And again, verily I say unto thy brethren, Sidney Rigdon and Frederick G. Williams, their sins are forgiven them also, and they are accounted as equal with thee in holding the keys of this last kingdom; as also through your administration the keys of the school of the prophets, which I have commanded to be organized, that thereby they may be perfected in their ministry for the *salvation of Zion*, and of the *nations of Israel*, and of the *Gentiles*, as many as will believe, that through your administration they may receive the word, and through their administration the word may go forth unto the ends of the earth, unto the Gentiles first, and then behold, and lo! they shall turn unto the Jews; and then cometh the day when the arm of the Lord shall be revealed in power in convincing the nations, the heathen nations, the house of Joseph, of the gospel of their salvation." 4th paragraph. "For it shall come to pass in that day, that every man shall hear the fulness of the gospel in his own tongue, and his own language, through those who are ordained unto this power, by the administration of the Comforter, and shed forth upon them for the revelation of Jesus Christ."

The foregoing revelations are of vast import in understanding the purpose of God as manifesting itself in his economy with his Zion. In the 3d paragraph we get the fact, that in bringing to pass the redemption of Zion, and preparing the way for the coming of the Savior, there were to be two dispensations under which all things were to be accomplished. In proof of this, we have the following said to Joseph Smith: "That through your ADMINISTRATION, they may receive the word, and through their ADMINISTRATION, the word may go forth to the ends of the earth."

Not only have we two administrations, but the work which belonged to each. Joseph Smith's administration was to bring forth the word; the other was to send the word to the ends of the earth. Two very different operations. It is under the second administration that Israel is to be gathered, and the way prepared for the coming of Christ. This fact is so clearly stated in the reference above as to leave no ground for cavil. In speaking of the priesthood which held the keys of the administration, the Spirit says: "And behold and lo! they shall turn unto the Jews." It is an important item, in this place, that Joseph Smith is not connected in the priesthood of the second dispensation at all, consequently, his priesthood did not belong to the second dispensation.

As we are speaking of the identity of the priesthood which is to gather Israel and prepare for the coming of Christ, we will copy from the Book of Mormon, 2d chapter of the 2d Book of Nephi, speaking of the seer: "Yet I will not loose his tongue, that he shall speak much; for I will not make him mighty in speaking. But I will write unto him my law, by the finger of mine own hand; and I will make for him a spokesman. And I, behold I will give unto him, that he shall write the writing of the fruit of thy loins, and the spokesman of thy loins shall declare it."

One priesthood was to bring forth the word of the Lord, for the benefit of the Lamanites, and the other priesthood was to proclaim it to them, and thereby save them. Nothing can be plainer than the case here is. He who held the keys of the first administration, was to bring forth the word, and he who held the keys of the second, was to gather them by means of that word. In connection with this, the 3d paragraph of the 95th section of the Book of Doctrine and Covenants says : "And it is expedient in me that you, my servant Sidney, should be a *spokesman* unto this people ; yea, verily, I will ordain you to this calling, even to be a spokesman unto my servant Joseph." The Lord had said, in the Book of Mormon, that he would raise up to Joseph Smith a spokesman ; and the Spirit said, in the Book of Doctrine and Covenants, that Sidney Rigdon was that spokesman. The case then stands thus : Joseph Smith was to translate the Book of Mormon, and Sidney Rigdon was to take it, and gather Israel.

Here is the sum of this whole matter. The prophet Malachi had said that before Christ came, he would send his messenger, and he should prepare the way before him. Joseph Smith said that Sidney Rigdon was that messenger. The Spirit said that the Lord would raise up a spokesman to Joseph Smith, and Joseph Smith said Sidney Rigdon was that spokesman. The Lord said he would prepare a priesthood with which he would gather Israel. Joseph Smith said that Sidney Rigdon held that priesthood.

The form of expression used about bringing this priesthood to light, certainly calls for a remark, in this place, from us. It was said to Oliver Cowdery and Joseph Smith, that they had the keys of the *gift* to bring this priesthood to light. Rather a singular form of expression: "*keys of a gift;*" but the case, as it transpired, gave great significance to the form of expression. We have seen in a former quotation, taken from the 11th section and 2d paragraph, that the priesthood in question, at the time the revelation was given to Joseph Smith and Oliver Cowdery, was only in the Divine mind; it had been communicated to no living person, not even to the one who had been sent forth to discharge its duties. Joseph Smith nor Oliver Cowdery had never heard tell of him who was to hold this priesthood; and the Lord said through Joseph Smith to Sidney Rigdon, that he had been sent forth as John, but *he* knew it not.

This was the position things were in, when Joseph Smith and Oliver Cowdery had the keys of the *gift* bestowed on them to bring the priesthood to light. Oliver Cowdery was the man who brought the Book of Mormon to Sidney Rigdon (entire strangers to each other), and presented it as a revelation, and asked him to give it a reading. He did so, and the Spirit of truth which was in him, pronounced it a revelation. The consequence was, that Oliver Cowdery baptized him, and he was introduced into the church. So that conjointly they brought the priesthood to light, and thus it was, they had the *keys of the gift;* that is, they had power given to them, conjointly, to bring to light a something which was alone in the mind of the Deity. They got the man, and then the Lord told Joseph Smith that this man was the person whom he had sent forth to prepare the way before him and Elijah which was to come.

As we have before ascertained that Joseph Smith's priesthood was not found in the books, identified with this last work of gathering together all things in one, there are other names identified with it. In section 39, paragraph 5, of Doctrine and Covenants, we read the following, given to David Whitmer: "Behold, I am Jesus Christ the Son of the living God, who created the heavens and the earth; a light which cannot be hid in darkness. Wherefore, I must bring forth the fulness of my gospel from the Gentiles unto the house of Israel. And behold, thou art David, and thou art called to assist: which thing if ye do, and are faithful, ye shall be blessed both spiritually and temporally, and great shall be your reward. Amen."

By this the original calling of David Whitmer was to assist in gathering Israel.

In the 46th section and 3d paragraph, we have the calling of Oliver Cowdery. After telling many things which pertained to him, the Spirit closes with telling him that he was to "be the first preacher of this church unto the church, and before the world; yea, before the Gentiles; yea, and thus saith the Lord God: lo! lo! to the Jews also. Amen."

This shows that Oliver Cowdery was called at first as one of those who should gather Israel.

Frederick G. Williams, as has been seen in a former quotation, was also called to this same work; but notwithstanding all these calls, when the time comes for the work to be done, there is but one found. " I will call on *one* of my servants to go and gather up the residue; and I will send my messenger, and he shall prepare the way before me;" not servants nor messengers.

Perhaps the words of Christ could never be more appropriately applied than they can in this case: "There are many called, but few chosen."

We may add here that if there are to be found hereditary priesthoods for the gathering of Israel, it is to one or all of these families to which reference must be had, and not to that of Joseph Smith; but this is just as people fancy: it has nothing to do with us; our business is to take the books, and be governed by them, and let others attend to as much outside business as they choose.

SECTION V.

There are some things in the 101st section and 3d paragraph of the Doctrine and Covenants, which pertains to the gathering of Israel, that should be called into view. " Behold, I say unto you, the redemption of Zion must needs come by power; therefore, I will raise up unto my people a man, who shall lead them like as Moses led the children of Israel; for ye are the children of Israel and of the seed of Abraham, and ye must needs be led out of bondage by power." These words are predicated on the fact that the church is in bondage, and when they come out, it will be by power, as Moses led the house of Israel.

Let us take, in connection with this, the 3d paragraph of the 85th section, which we have already referred to. In speaking of the mission of Sidney Rigdon, as connected with Frederick G. Williams, we have these words: "And then behold, and lo, they shall turn to the Jews; and then cometh the day when the arm of the Lord shall be revealed in power, in convincing the nations, the heathen nations, the house of Joseph, of the gospel of their salvation." 4th paragraph. "For it shall come to pass in that day, that every man shall hear the fulness of the gospel in his own tongue, and his own language, through those who are ordained unto this power by the administration of the Comforter, and shed forth upon them, for the revelation of Jesus Christ."

Here we are told who the man is who is to lead Zion like Moses did Israel. It is said of Sidney Rigdon, that when the ministry he holds shall turn to the Jews, then cometh the day when the "arm of the Lord shall be revealed in *power;*" so if Zion is to be led by power, he is the man that is to do it; and if the arm of the Lord is not to be revealed in power till he turns to the Jews, then no other man can do it; and if this is not the case, the book is not intelligible. The case then stands thus: Joseph Smith, in his revelations, says that Zion has to be led, in order for her redemption, by power, as Moses led Israel; and then says that Sidney Rigdon is that man. And then after telling, in the 4th paragraph, how that power would be manifested, " that every man should hear the fulness of the gospel in his own language," he further says that this power should manifest itself through those who were ordained unto it, through the administration of the Comforter, and shed forth upon them, "*for the revelation of Jesus Christ.*" The *revelation* of Jesus Christ is a form of expression used to denote his second coming. For this we refer the reader to the first chapter of 2d Thessalonians, 7th and 8th verses, where the apostle says: "And to you who are troubled, rest with us, when the Lord Jesus shall be *revealed* from heaven with his mighty angels, in flaming fire, taking vengeance on them that know not God," &c.

Surely controversy here ends, and the matter presents itself clearly and forcibly, that Sidney Rigdon has been called, ordained and qualified to redeem Zion by power, and thereby preparing the way for the *revelation* or second coming of Christ.

There are some declarations in the 3d paragraph of the 95th section, from whence we have been copying, though it may seem rather like an episode than a continuation of the subject, yet, as they are important, we are disposed to give them a place here. It is where the Spirit was making known the mission of Sidney Rigdon. It is said, that "the arm of the Lord shall be revealed in power in convincing the nations, the heathen nations, the house of Joseph, of the gospel of their salvation."

It can no longer be a doubt but that Sidney Rigdon is the Lord's agent to bring the Lamanites to the knowledge of the gospel of their salvation. The house of Joseph refers to the Lamanites. But the manner in which it is introduced here is somewhat peculiar, and throws light upon a great subject. The phrase to which we allude, is the "heathen nations, the house of Joseph." In thus speaking, there is light thrown upon the subject as found in the 2d Psalm and 8th verse, where it is said: "Ask of me, and I will give thee the heathen for thine inheritance, and the uttermost parts of the earth for thy possession." All sectariandom have been trying to convert the heathen throughout the world, to bring in the millennium. But here we learn the important fact that what Christ was to have for an inheritance, was the house of Joseph, and this is confirmed by connecting it with the uttermost parts of the earth, and that is this continent; for this continent is the uttermost parts of the earth, from where the prophecy was delivered.

This revelation of Joseph Smith obviates a great difficulty which must exist, otherwise, on the mind of every Biblical student; for the prophets of the Old Testament, in speaking of the recovery of Israel, and the redemption of Zion, also pronounce judgment upon the old Gentile heathen, instead of giving them to the Lord for an inheritance. In the 149th Psalm, 7th, 8th and 9th verses, the Psalmist says of the Gentile heathen (he is writing on the restoration of Israel): "To execute *vengeance* upon the heathen, and punishment upon the people. 8th. To bind their kings with chains, and their nobles with fetters of iron; 9th. To execute upon them the judgment *written*." And in the Prophecy of Micah, 5th chapter and 15th verse, the prophet declares the Lord will " execute vengeance in anger and fury upon the heathen, such as they have not known." Not very much like their being the Lord's heritage.

Our Book of Doctrine and Covenants comes happily to our relief, and informs us that it was the heathenized house of Joseph that was given to the Lord for his inheritance. And we are assured that, through the administration of Sidney Rigdon, they will receive the gospel of their salvation, and become the Lord's inheritance; and by these means the Lord will possess himself of the uttermost parts of the earth.

All controversy here ends, and doubt disappears about Sidney Rigdon being the messenger of the Lord, to redeem the house of Joseph and recover the tribes of Jacob, and prepare the way for the coming of the Lord.

As we have seen that under the administration of the gathering the Lord would reveal his arm in power, let us refer to what is said on the subject. In the 11th section and 3d paragraph of Doctrine and Covenants, the Spirit says: "And it shall come to pass, that there shall be a great work in the land, even among the Gentiles, for their folly and abominations shall be made manifest in the eyes of all people: for I am God, and mine arm is not shortened, and I will show miracles, signs and wonders unto all those who believe on my name. And whoso shall ask it in my name, in faith, they shall cast out devils; they shall heal the sick; they shall cause the blind to receive their sight, and the deaf to hear, and dumb to speak, and the lame to walk: and the time speedily cometh that great things are to be shown forth unto the children of men."

The above was written by Joseph Smith to Sidney Rigdon in relation to the work of preparing, and not in relation to the work then in operation. The declaration "that the time speedily cometh that great things are to be shown forth unto the children of men," refers, certainly, to a future time, and not the time then when the revelation was written; for had it referred to the time when the revelation was written, it would have said: "The time has come when great things will be shown forth to the children of men," instead of saying, "the time speedily cometh;" but as it was written immediately in connection with the enunciation of the mission to prepare the way for the coming of Christ, its referring to that time as "the time that speedily cometh," none but a caviller would dispute. The whole of the section relates to the same time for its fulfilment. There are some things said in the 6th paragraph, which puts the case even beyond a caviller. "Keep all the commandments and covenants by which you are bound, and I will cause the heavens to shake for your good, and Satan shall tremble." Surely these things remain to this day unfulfilled, and will remain so till the priesthood appointed to prepare the way, turns to the Jews, and the arm of the Lord is revealed in power.

The grand and majestic saying, "I will shake the heavens for your good," will get a great significance by turning to the old prophets; for we are required to study them as well as the Books of Mormon and Covenants. This promise, as we have it, is based upon the prophecies of the old prophets from the deepest antiquity; from two to three thousand years back among the ancients. See Joel, 3d chapter, 16th verse; Haggai, 2d chapter, 6th verse. Based on these prophecies, we have the apostolic promise in Hebrews, 12th chapter, 26th verse. With the old prophetic writers it was delivered as a prophecy, but the apostle gives it to us as a promise. "The Lord hath promised," &c.

So stood the prophecy and promise among the holy men of old, but to us it has assumed a more definite character. To them it was a future event, time indefinite;

but to us it comes in a different way; it is a promise made to an individual; calling him by name and saying, it shall be done, "*for your good.*" The subject of this promise is the only one on this earth to whom this prophecy of antiquity has been individually applied. In regard to this most majestic of all promises, we have a great advantage over our brethren of former days. Here is the man now living among us to whom the promise is made, and he is assured that it shall be done for *his* good: thus bringing the fulfilment of it to our day. To them it was an indefinite promise of the future. To us a definite one of the present. The man is now living, and the only one to whom the promise is made; and the only one to whom it was ever made individually, and within the limits of whose ministration it was to be fulfilled.

If some should suppose, by reading the whole revelation, that Joseph Smith was united in the promise, to this all we need say, if it were, then it makes him a covenant-breaker; for it came from his own lips, to "keep the commandments and *covenants* by which ye are bound, and I WILL CAUSE THE HEAVENS TO SHAKE FOR YOUR GOOD." Joseph Smith is gone, and if he were included in the promise, he did not keep the commandments and covenants as required, or else the promise is false.

Inasmuch, however, as we have not found Joseph Smith's name identified with the work of preparing the way for the coming of Christ, it is not to be supposed that the Spirit of revelation intended to include his name in the promise.

It may not be improper to remark, in this place, that the 11th section from which we are now copying, was delivered by Joseph Smith to and concerning Sidney Rigdon, as the substance of it shows. In the 5th paragraph, it is said to Sidney Rigdon that the Lord's elect or covenant seed will hear his voice, and shall see him, and shall not be asleep, and shall abide the day of his coming, "for they shall be purified, even as I am pure." Thus speaks the Spirit to Sidney Rigdon concerning the glory of his mission, which is to prepare the way of Christ's coming; and hence it is said to him, concerning the covenant seed, that they shall abide the day of Christ's coming.

What is said in this 5th paragraph about the Lord's elect being pure as he is pure, requires a farther notice. In the 82d section and 5th paragraph, we read: "Therefore, verily thus saith the Lord, Let Zion rejoice, for this is Zion, THE PURE IN HEART."

Zion then is the pure in heart, and we are told the people of the Lord under the administration of Sidney Rigdon, will be pure as the Lord is pure; and as this is never said concerning the administration of any other, it makes him the head of Zion, and under his administration is Zion to exist and nowhere else.

It is of importance that we keep in mind the great assurance given, that *all* the prophecies and promises in the Book of Doctrine and Covenants will be fulfilled, and if so, the multitude to which we have referred are of the number. A recapitulation will be of interest here. That there is a man pointed out, called by name, and his mission clearly and incontrovertibly established, around whom nearly all the promises in the book cluster, is indisputable to any and all who take the books for their guide. He is to prepare the way for the coming of the Savior and Elijah. Through his administration the heathenized house of Joseph or Lamanites are to receive the gospel of their salvation; through his administration the house of Israel is to be gathered; under his administration the arm of the Lord is to be revealed in power. The nations are to hear the gospel in their own language. Under his administration the sick are to be healed; the deaf hear; the lame walk; the blind see, and devils be cast out, and the heavens are to shake for his good. Zion is to rejoice in her redemption, and to be thrown down no more forever. All this through the guidance and rule of the one man, Sidney Rigdon. Now we ask, Are all these prophecies and promises to be fulfilled? If they are not, then the Books of Mormon and Doctrine and Covenants are a mass of abominations, such as never came forth from the lips of any other man that ever lived. But we believe they will be fulfilled; yea, we almost, if not altogether, say we know it; for we have had things manifested in connection with the sending forth of this our appeal, which puts the subject at rest in our hearts.

Let our readers pause and ask themselves, when the commission of Sidney Rigdon is executed, as in accordance with the prophecies and promises in the books, Where is the place for any other man? What is there for him to do in relation to Zion? and we think he will answer to himself, that there is nothing any other man can do. Zion is to be in all her departments and powers under the presidency of that one man.

What is Brigham Young doing, or what can he do?

We answer, Just what he is doing, as testified by Joseph Smith : working out his own overthrow and the destruction of those who are led by him.

Or, what can young Joseph Smith do? There is but one thing he can do or will do : he can curse his father's memory into everlasting infamy by bringing into discredit all he has caused to be written; for, if the position he occupies is true, his father was the greatest falsifier that ever lived. This all must see who read the books he has published. As far then as his influence goes, so far will contempt be cast upon the memory of his father; for all the promises and prophecies of his father will fail. We will here refer to one of the books of his father's to show what fate awaits him. We copy from the 12th chapter of the last Nephi, as follows: "And if it so be that the church is built upon my gospel, then will the Father show forth his own works in it." We have seen where the Father said he would show forth his works, through the administration of Sidney Rigdon. " But if it be not built upon my gospel, and is built upon the works of men, or of devils, verily I say unto you, they have joy in their works for a season, and by and by the end cometh, and they are hewn down and cast into the fire, from whence there is no return." So the son deals with his father; and so the father disposes of his son. The son consigns the memory of his father to everlasting infamy, and the father dooms his son to eternal perdition; and there we leave them, and close this section.

SECTION VI.

We commence this division of our appeal by transferring into it a part of the 3d paragraph of the 85th section of Doctrine and Covenants. Speaking to Joseph Smith, the Spirit says of Sidney Rigdon and Frederick G. Williams: "And they are accounted as equal with thee in holding the keys of this last kingdom: as also through your administration the keys of the school of the prophets, which I have commanded to be organized, that thereby they may be *perfected* in their ministry for the salvation of Zion, and the nations of Israel, and of the Gentiles, as many as will believe, that through your administration they may receive the word, and through their administration the word may go forth to the ends of the earth," &c. Let us just say here that F. G. Williams, whose name is found in this quotation, some time after this was written fell from his steadfastness, and not long after that, into his grave, and ended his career.

From the above, the fact is disclosed, that the priesthood there spoken of, had to be *perfected*, in order that it might carry the gospel to the ends of the earth for the salvation of all, both Jew and Gentile. The inquiry now arises, How was that to be done? The keys of the kingdom and the school of the prophets were given, that thereby they might *perfect* their ministry, which had to be done before they could go forth in the power of it; for we have seen that *power* was to accompany its execution. How, then, was it to be perfected? For an answer to this we will begin by referring the reader to the 7th section of Doctrine and Covenants, and 21st paragraph, which is in the language following: "Also, I give unto you a commandment, that ye shall continue in prayer and fasting from this time forth. And I give unto you a commandment, that you shall teach one another the doctrine of the kingdom; teach ye diligently, and my grace shall attend you, that you may be instructed more perfectly in theory, in principle, in doctrine, in the law of the gospel, in all things that pertain unto the kingdom of God, that is expedient for you to understand; of things, both in heaven, and in earth, and under the earth; things which have been; things which are; things which must shortly come to pass; things which are at home; things which are abroad; the wars and perplexities of the nations; and the judgments which are in the land; and a knowledge also of countries, and of kingdoms, that ye may be prepared in all things when I shall send you again, to magnify the calling whereunto I have called you, and mission with which I have commissioned you."

Here, then, is a field of intelligence to explore, which pertains to the qualifications of the priesthood; and these requirements are made for the purpose of enabling the priesthood "*to magnify their calling.*"

These magnificent duties cover the entire learning of the world; that if a priesthood is perfected before God, it must have in possession, not only the literature which belongs to the doctrine of Christ, but that of the world also. All these acquirements are subordinate to a grand object, as here declared: "*That ye may be prepared in all things, when I shall send you again, to magnify the calling whereunto I have called you, and mission with which I have commissioned you.*" The same as to say, If you do not acquire the intelligence here required, you cannot *magnify* your calling.

In connection with the above are some important declarations found in the 12th paragraph of the 83d section, where the duties required, as stated above, are specially demanded of three persons, namely Joseph Smith, Sidney Rigdon and Frederick G. Williams. "And verily I say unto you, that it is my will that you should hasten to translate my Scriptures, and to obtain a knowledge of history, and of countries, and of kingdoms, of laws of God and man; and all this *for the salvation of Zion.*" The subject, as enforced by the last quotation, assumes a commanding character; a something not to be dispensed with, for they are essential for the *salvation* of Zion: implying that without these qualifications in the priesthood, Zion cannot be saved. From all these facts put together, Zion can never be redeemed until her priesthood possess the knowledge and intelligence as required above. It is a matter of no small consequence to have such questions as these clearly settled; for an error here is fatal. Should we be so unfortunate as to be flattering ourselves that we are engaged in the work of saving Zion, when the priesthood by which we are led are destitute of the literature required by the Spirit of revelation, in the end we shall be hewn down and cast into the fire, for all those things have been required of the priesthood, for *the salvation of Zion.* Where those qualifications do not exist, there Zion is not.

Nothing can strike the mind with more force than the

enjoining on the priesthood of Zion, duties of such extent pertaining to erudition. The priesthood which the Lord ordains for the redemption of his Zion, must be able to silence the world on their own principles, with their own learning, apart from the sublime and profound intelligence which belongs to the priesthood only.

In making the requirement to which we have been referring, *special*, and demanding it of three men, and these called by name, there are two implications equally as strong as the declaration. One is, that without the required intelligence Zion could not be saved; and the other is, that the salvation of Zion was to be brought to pass through and by these men. It is said concerning *them, not others*, "that it is my will *you* should do it for the salvation of Zion." The conclusion of the whole matter is, that the learning of the world to a high degree, not to say superlative degree, must be possessed by the priesthood of Zion, in order for her salvation. A sentence from the 3d paragraph of the 85th section will put this case in a light which admits of no doubt. Speaking to Joseph Smith, concerning Sidney Rigdon and F. G. Williams, the Spirit says: "And they are accounted as equal with thee in holding the keys of this last kingdom; as also through your administration the keys of the school of the prophets, which I have commanded to be organized, that thereby they may be perfected in their ministry *for the salvation of Zion.*" The same that is said concerning their obtaining the learning of the world: it was *for the salvation of Zion.* Leaving no ground for mistake, that from and through them the *salvation* of Zion was to come.

Not only was there a high degree of literature, such as belongs to the world generally, required of the priesthood through which Zion was to be saved, but an unequalled degree of the sacred literature of the Scriptures also, which is found written most impressively in the Book of Doctrine and Covenants, 95th section and 3d paragraph, and are such as these: "And it is expedient in me that you, my servant Sidney, should be a spokesman unto this people; yea, verily, I will ordain you unto this calling, even to be a spokesman unto my servant Joseph; and I will give unto him power to be mighty in testimony; and I will give unto thee power to be mighty in expounding all Scriptures, that thou *mayest be* a spokesman unto him, and he shall be a revelator unto thee, that thou mayest know the *certainty* of all things pertaining to the things of my kingdom on earth."

There is a sentence in the sayings here recorded that calls for a special notice. Where it is said to Sidney Rigdon: "And I will give unto thee power to be mighty in expounding all Scriptures, that thou *mayest be* a *spokesman* unto him." From these declarations it is manifest that to be a spokesman, a man must be able to expound all Scriptures, or else the Spirit would not have said, "I will give thee power to expound all Scriptures," that thou *mayest be a spokesman:* the same as to say, that unless thou canst expound all Scriptures, thou canst not be a *spokesman;* and another implication is equally manifest: that if not able to be a spokesman, then, thou canst not take the words of the Nephites, and declare them to the Lamanites, for this required a *spokesman.* Thus establishing the fact, that unless a man can expound all Scriptures, he cannot convince the house of Joseph of the gospel of their salvation. But this last implication is still stronger, and that is, unless the Spirit thus qualifies a man, the whole scheme of gathering Israel would prove a failure.

Who cannot understand, that all the learning thus required would want years in order to obtain it, a literature of a higher degree than that which is common to the world, besides the sacred learning which is peculiar to the priesthood? Indeed, when we read these things, we say in our heart, Who is sufficient for them? We presume to answer, No other man, only he of whom the requirement is made. How will a man be *able* to expound *all* Scriptures, not to say, be *mighty* to do it? for that implies perfection in his attainments, and corresponds exactly with the duty of *perfecting* his ministry: the thing that is said he should do. He should *perfect* his ministry, by being *perfect* in expounding *all* Scriptures.

Those who will ponder and reflect, will see a cause for things that would, without this, be inexplicable. Who cannot comprehend that it would take years after years to enable any man to acquire the erudition included in this field of survey, particularly when he is told how it had to be obtained, through books; for there was no other way to get it. How long would it take a person to make himself acquainted with history, and with countries, and with kingdoms, of laws of God and man? Surely a series of years.

The books give us a clue to the time it would take. Take Moses, for example. We are told that he was learned in all the learning of the Egyptians; that is, he was learned in the learning of the world, and that he spent forty years in Egypt to do it, and then he fled to the land of Midian, and there he found Jethro, who was a man holding the priesthood (see 4th section of Book of Doctrine and Covenants, 2d paragraph), and there he was for forty years more getting the peculiar learning which belonged to the priesthood only; in all, eighty years. Now the intelligence which the Lord requires of him who holds the priesthood of the preparation, is precisely of the same character,—the learning of the world and that of the priesthood. If then it took Moses eighty years, how long would it take Sidney Rigdon to obtain the same knowledge? Let the reader judge for himself.

There is a point now reached, that requires comparing things with each other.

Since the death of Joseph Smith, what have men been at? Making prophets for themselves, as the Israelites made the calf in the wilderness. Youngs rose up, imitating the voice of Joseph Smith, and mimicking his actions, claiming that the spirit of Smith had entered him, and that he had become what the heathens called an Avatar. The very means used by them with which to introduce idolatry in the first instance. This wizardly business took with it great multitudes. Strang dug plates, and got records thereby. Bencemy discovered that the gospel had not yet been preached in power as it would be when the Lord gathered Israel. On this he organized his congregation. But from these strange works of men, let us turn and see what the Lord was doing. Before we do that let us barely notice the last of all these efforts of human folly,—the appearance of young Smith with his hereditary priesthood. The Lord had said that he did not " walk in crooked paths; neither did he turn to the right hand or left ;" and so the sequel will prove; for he proceeded as he had said he would. He had separated unto himself, taking him out of the midst of that people, bent on folly, a priesthood, which he had said he would qualify, for the purpose of leading Zion to her deliverance and salvation, and according to his word, he placed him in a situation for that purpose; making him acquainted with the literature of the world as he had required, and with that of the priesthood, as he had promised, and it was here the Lord was working, and nowhere else, and at this he continued to work, turning neither to the right hand or left, but fulfilling his own word, and sustaining his own promise, and qualifying his own priesthood, which he had chosen, and not man. Satan, however, had determined that such an event as qualifying the Lord's priesthood, never should take place; for, as he had got the Smith family under his influence, he turned them on to the one the Lord had chosen, with a fury that might have done honor to Saul when he sought the life of David. Saul would not, however, have condescended to the scandalous degradation of the Smith family. Saul was a man who had been too well raised to condescend to the low vulgarity of the Smiths. Such outrages as they committed were peculiar to the lowest class of mankind.

What presents the case now under consideration in its most forbidding character was, that the revilers and persecutors, in this instance, were more indebted to the persecuted for the position they occupied than all the rest put together; but when a people fall from their steadfastness before God, and give themselves over to Satan, they are far worse than those who had never known God. Consequently, there was no falsehood too foul for Joseph and his wife to fabricate; no slander too base for their foul and polluted hearts to invent; no degraded condescension too low for them to bow to in order to effect their demoniacal purpose of destroying their benefactor; and when they could do nothing else, they attacked his family, trying to scandalize two or three innocent girls. They employed all over whom they had any influence. Persons went off a distance, and wrote back that they had there found letters written by his family speaking evil of the Smiths; the whole concocted among themselves, to create some excuse for their sardonic falsehoods. Men were employed to bear false witness, and perjure themselves to effect their object.

As far as the Lord's chosen was concerned, he had to suffer it, to fulfil a prophecy of Isaiah, which was transferred into the Book of Mormon, that had been fulfilled in the person of the Lord himself; but it was put into the Book of Mormon to let us know that it had to be fulfilled in connection with the coming forth of that book. It is in the 40th chapter, and begins with the 3d verse, as follows: "He shall not cry nor lift up, nor cause his voice to be heard in the street. A bruised reed shall he not break, and the smoking flax shall he not quench; he shall bring forth judgment into victory."

It was to fulfil this prophecy upon the head of the Lord's chosen, that he and his family were subjected to the fiendish corruption of the Smith family and their coadjutors, the twelve; and it was never more perfectly fulfilled on the head of the Savior than it was on the head of his servant. Let the attentive reader consult the 12th chapter of Matthew, where we have the account of its fulfilment in the person of Christ, and compare the two cases as fulfilled on the head of his servant, and he will find them correspond in every respect. Christ pursued his course, interfering with no person's business but his own; he was followed by the revilings and persecutions of his enemies without a response from him, and this is said, by the sacred writer, to fulfil the prophecy to which we are referring. In relation to his servant, it was the very same : he was silent, and let them rage and foam out their fiendish corruption. He let it all pass by in silence, until even his persecutors and defamers of his family, became ashamed. And thus the prophecy of Isaiah has actually had its fulfilment in the person of Sidney Rigdon; letting all know that he is the Lord's servant to the exclusion of all others.

At this period, the salvation of Zion depended entirely on the firmness and Christ-like condition of one man. Had he been overcome, all would have been lost; but his endurance, "as seeing Him who is invisible," baffled Satan, and foiled him in his determination to stop the progress of truth.

He had got the Smith family, as facts afterwards proved, and through them the twelve "*blasphemers*" got power to get the control of the church; and the end will be the prophecy of Joseph Smith, that "few of them would stand to get an inheritance."

We who send forth this appeal were knowing, personally, to the scandalous outrages committed by the Smith family against the Lord's chosen and his family. We were there and saw it and heard it, and the falsifying and slandering of the Smith family were more like fiends than human beings, while it was known to all who chose to know, that the abused family had given no cause for it, but had been the friends of the revilers and persecutors. The entire cause was that the Smith family had yielded themselves up to Satan to do his will.

In giving this account, we say, as did John the Apostle, " What we saw and heard, this we declare unto you."

But now for the sequel. After the Lord had given Satan full power, as he had in the case of Job, and the prophecy had been fulfilled to the very letter, and his servant had acted as he had done himself, when tried in the same way, he took his servant and his family, and led them quietly away. But now for what followed. They had not been gone but a few days, when vengeance overtook the transgressors to the uttermost: the Smith family was hurled down, as with fury. Joseph and Hiram were both killed, and Samuel died; sweeping the family with a desolation as great or greater than the rejected houses of Saul or Eli.

Thus we saw transgressors act, and thus we saw the Lord act; and saw the house of Smith hurled down by . one blast of Divine wrath.

After the overthrow of the Smith family, the twelve stepped into their footsteps, and began to slander and vilify the same family, and as causelessly as the Smiths had done it, and equally as base and vulgar and fiendish.

And again the Lord showed himself in his wrath against them: they were driven out as by a tempest, and sent entirely away out of the land of Zion, there to await the destruction to which the prophecy of Joseph Smith had doomed them. Surely, "the way of transgressors is hard."

It may not be amiss here to call into view some important facts as written, concerning the falling of prophets by their being overcome by the adversary; that we may see that Joseph Smith was not the only prophet which has fallen by transgression. There are declarations found in the 14th chapter of Ezekiel, which are positive in the case. We recommend the careful reading of the whole chapter, but particularly the 9th and 10th verses. In the Book of Mormon also, the same principles are recognized. It is said of the seed of Christ (Book of Mosiah, chapter 8th), "Yea, and are not the prophets, every one that has opened his mouth to prophesy, that has not *fallen into transgression;* I mean all the *holy prophets* ever since the world began." This language speaks for itself, that prophets are as liable to fall by transgression as any other; even Elias, who could stay the heaven, was *subject* to passions like other men, and, consequently, as liable to fall. In the 24th chapter of Matthew, we have the whole case, in language not to be mistaken; and the case now under consideration portrayed exactly. We begin with the 46th verse: "Blessed is that servant whom his Lord, when he cometh, shall find so doing; verily, I say unto you, that he shall make him ruler over all his goods; but, and if that evil servant shall say in his heart, My Lord delayeth his coming, and shall begin to smite his fellow-servants, and to eat and drink with the drunken, the Lord of that servant shall come in a day when he looketh not for him, and an hour that he is not aware of, and cut him asunder, and appoint him his portion with the hypocrites. There shall be weeping," &c.

This quotation settles the whole question, for it is a case in point, and shows it could not be otherwise than that Joseph Smith should be cut off; for if there ever was a man who got to eating and drinking with the drunken, Joseph Smith was one. Not only did he eat and drink *with* the drunken, but got drunk himself, and abused his fellow-servants to the extent of his power, and that without any regard to truth, and taught those over whom he had influence, that they ought to lie for him; and Parley P. Pratt, who has, since Smith was cut off, shared a similar fate himself, and for the same cause, that of transgression, had the boldness once to say that they ought to lie for Brother Joseph; and it was a fact that he and others did so on the grand scale.

However strange it may appear to those who are ignorant of the Lord's way of dealing with mankind, that all these events go to prove that Joseph Smith was in reality what he professed to be, the Lord's servant, the fact that the Lord cut him off, exactly according to the law he had given concerning his own servants, would prove that, if nothing else would do it. There could be no more unlikely thing, than that the Lord would deal with an impostor in exact accordance with the law he had published concerning his own servants. Had Joseph Smith not have been the Lord's servant, he might have eat and drank with the drunken, and smote his fellow-servants till this day, as far as the Lord was concerned; but being his servant, he dealt with him as such, and cut him off. Thus making his death prove what his life went to contradict.

Leaving this part of the subject here, we proceed to consult the books upon the subject of the fulfilment of prophecy, as connected with the Lord's messenger. In the preceding part of this appeal, it has been clearly understood, the way the Lord took to perfect his priesthood, by literature of the highest order. Isaiah has a saying that gives additional strength to these literary acquirements. We take as transferred into the Book of Mormon, 2d Nephi, 5th chapter, where the prophet said the Lord would give to his servant "the tongue of the learned." Its being transferred into the Book of Mormon, shows that this giving of the tongue of the learned, was to take place in connection with the coming forth of that book. The extensive literature that had to be obtained by the priesthood was, as we here see, to fulfil a prophecy; and also what is said in 95th section, 3d paragraph of the Book of Doctrine and Covenants, that when his servant turned to the Jews, the arm of the Lord would be revealed in power, has its connection and basis in the prophecy of Isaiah. Such as the following: "The Lord will make bare his arm in the sight of all nations, and the ends of the earth shall see the salvation of God." And again: "Awake! awake! Put on strength, O! arm of the Lord!" As also, "Mine arm judge the people." All of the above are transferred to the Book of Mormon.

It is by reason of the connection with these old prophecies, that what the Lord says concerning Sidney Rigdon's turning to the Jews, and the arm of the Lord being revealed in power, that give that promise to him its great consequence; for it was to be in consequence of this revealing of the arm of the Lord that the entire deliverance was to come to Israel. Everything which the Lord had ever promised Israel, was subordinate to his making bare his arm in the eyes of the nations. These old prophecies and promises, which have been lying on the pages of sacred history for thousands of years, are suddenly started into a vigorous life, by the all-important annunciation that the Lord has a priesthood chosen, ordained, and qualified, through whose administration the long-promised event of the arm of the Lord being revealed, is to be fulfilled. The man is now prepared to commence the great work, by which the arm of the Lord is to be revealed in power, the heavens to be shaken, and Israel to be gathered from the four quarters of the earth.

The sublimity and grandeur of these astounding facts, are greatly increased by marking well that these promises were all made to the Jews, and pertained to their gathering. It was to the Jews, in relation to their being gathered, that the arm of the Lord was to be revealed; the heavens were to be shaken, and the tongue of the learned was to be given to his messenger, who was to gather their scattered tribes. Putting the case beyond the possibility of doubt, that Sidney Rigdon is the Lord's messenger to recover the tribes of Jacob; for the Lord has clustered all these promises around him and none other.

There are other things said by Isaiah, which are important to be called into view here. They, too, are transferred into the Book of Mormon, to let us know that their fulfilment belongs to their gathering. 2d Book of Nephi, 9th chapter: "And there shall come forth a rod out of the stem of Jesse, and a branch shall grow out of his roots; and the Spirit of the Lord shall rest upon him, the spirit of wisdom and understanding, the spirit of counsel and might, the spirit of knowledge and of the fear of the Lord; and shall make him of quick understanding in the fear of the Lord; and he shall not judge after the sight of his eyes, neither reprove after the hearing of his ears; but with righteousness shall he judge the poor, and reprove with equity for the meek of the earth; and he shall smite the earth with the rod of his mouth, and with the breath of his lips shall he slay the wicked. And righteousness shall be the girdle of his loins, and faithfulness the girdle of his reins." And then we are told that the wolf and the lamb shall dwell together, &c. And it is then farther said, "And in that day there shall be a root of Jesse, which shall stand for an ensign of the people; to it shall the Gentiles seek, and his rest shall be glorious." After all this is said, the time is fixed for its accomplishment. "And it shall come to pass in that day, that the Lord shall set his hand again the second time to recover the remnant of his people." The prophet proceeds to inform us of the countries from whence Israel shall be gathered.

The query arises about this branch out of the root of Jesse, as well as the root itself. That they both refer to Christ need not be doubted; but that the time when this rule of righteousness shall be exercised, which is here stated to be in connection with the gathering of Israel, settles the question that Christ himself will not be here; because he is not to come till after Israel is gathered. How then will this rule take place? To answer this question, we, as usual, appeal to the books. Moses said to the Jews, "that a prophet would the Lord their God raise up unto them like unto himself, and him should they hear." All the books say that the prophet here spoken of was Christ. By saying so, they made Christ like Moses. In our Book of Doctrine and Covenants, Christ says that he would raise up a man to lead his people by power, like Moses. Put all this together, and let us see to what it amounts. By it Christ is said to be like Moses, and if Christ raises up a man to lead Israel like Moses, then he raises a man like himself, for he is like Moses, and another man like Moses would be like Christ: the result of all is, that Christ is to raise a man to redeem Israel that will represent himself, will be a personification of himself, and will rule and direct the affairs of his kingdom exactly as he would do it, if he were in person. And so comes the rule of righteousness on the earth, before Christ comes, so that when the prophet Isaiah says: "There shall come forth a rod out of the stem of Jesse, and a branch shall grow out of his roots; and the Spirit of the Lord shall rest upon him," &c., all this righteousness and peace will be exercised by and through a man, whom the Lord has chosen for the purpose; yea, the very man whom he has called to prepare the way before him; and his having this transferred into the Book of Mormon, was for the express purpose of letting us know this important fact.

From all the prophecies and promises which are extant,

that the Lord has authorized us to believe, a question is so perfectly settled as to be put beyond the possibility of doubt, that Sidney Rigdon has been chosen and separated to the work of the Lord, for the purpose of recovering the tribes of Jacob as well as for the salvation of Zion, and that he is so to the exclusion of all others, and that all other pretenders are blasphemers, whose end is destruction, not only to themselves, but to all who will follow them. But this will appear in greater force and power, when we bring into view the place which prophesying occupies in the work of the Lord, as it is found written in the books; which brings us to the seventh section of our book.

SECTION VII.

As usual, we begin this section with an appeal to the books. Hear what Isaiah says. We take the words of Isaiah as found in the Book of Mormon, 6th chapter of the first Book of Nephi. We are told why it was that the Lord commenced his work by prophecy. Hear what he says: "Behold, I have declared the former things from the beginning; and they went forth out of my mouth, and I showed them. I did show them suddenly; and I did it, because I knew that thou art obstinate, and thy neck was an iron sinew, and thy brow brass; and I have, even from the beginning, declared them to thee; before it came to pass, I showed them to thee; and I showed them, for fear lest thou shouldest say, Mine idol hath done them, and my graven image and my molten image hath commanded them. Thou hast seen and heard all this; and will you not declare them? And that I have showed thee new things, from this time, even hidden things, and thou didst not know them. They are created now, and not from the beginning; even before the day when thou heardst them not, they were declared unto thee, lest thou shouldest say, Behold I knew them."

In the above quotation we have the whole subject embraced, showing why it was that the Lord raised up and sent forth prophets to foretell his work before it transpired: it was that those to whom the prophecies were delivered, might know what the work of the Lord was, in opposition to all others. It was to guard the people against imposition and impostures of all kinds. Before the Lord commenced his work among a people, he sent forth prophets to declare what he was going to do; so that when he prosecuted his work, all might have prophecy to direct them, so they need not be led astray.

In consequence of this, all were required to read that prophetic word, to study it and rely upon it; and not depart from it, because the Lord would fulfil his prophecies and promises which he had made; *he* would abide by his word, let us do as we might.

It is declared by the prophet that the Lord did so from the beginning; it was his established and continued policy with men, from which he never departed; and by these means, we are directed to look for the Lord, and to know that a work is his, because it was and is in fulfilment of prophecy. To the truth of this order of things, Amos the prophet adds his testimony, 3d chapter and 7th verse: "Surely the Lord God will do nothing, but he revealeth his secret unto his servants the prophets."

Those testimonies of the prophets put an end to all strife. In obedience to this uniform order of dealing, the Lord begins his work by first raising up and sending a prophet to make known what he is going to do, and how he is going to do it; and last, but not least, by whom he is going to do it; and when he commences to work, he begins in obedience to his unchangeable order; and all he does is in fulfilment of the prophecies which he has caused to be written in relation to it. He says he does this that men may know that it is even he who is working, for he challenges Satan and all his hosts to work according to that rule. In thus working by a law which none other but himself can work by, he convinces, as he goes, all who are capable of understanding, that it is the Lord himself who is working; and thus he establishes his character and influence in the world.

He gave us notice, at the commencement of his work with us, that in dealing with us, he was going to proceed on the same principle, as we learn from the books. In the Book of Mormon, first Book of Nephi, 3d chapter, Nephi discourses thus: "For he is the same yesterday, to-day, and forever; and the way is prepared from the foundation of the world, if it so be that they repent and come to him; for he that diligently seeketh, shall find; and the mysteries of God shall be unfolded unto them by the power of the Holy Ghost, as well in these times as in times of old, and as well in times of old as in times to come; wherefore the course of the Lord is one eternal round." The same form of expression is found in different places in the Book of Doctrine and Covenants, by which we learn that the policy he had pursued from the beginning should be continued with us, and that he would be governed by the same rule. And as he had condemned the people, in all ages, who rejected the revelations he gave, and the teachings of the prophets he sent to them, so he, in like manner, would condemn us. Here we have overwhelming force given to the requirement made of us, by assuring us that we were all under condemnation, and should remain so till we turned to the Book of Mormon and former commandments we had received.

Having brought with us the prophecies and promises written and published by Joseph Smith, we have come to a knowledge of his mission by virtue of his own writings, without any conjectures or opinions of ourselves or others. He was sent of the Lord as prophet and revelator to inform the Gentiles the Lord was preparing to do a great and marvellous work, that would either prove to their salvation or condemnation ; and, prophetically, to make known the great events connected with it, and to let us all understand that unless we gave diligent heed to the requirements of heaven, we should perish in the general ruin ; as also to bring to light the priesthood, through and by whose administration the great and marvellous work would be brought to pass, and give instructions and directions in relation to giving such notice of the great coming work to the Gentiles, as the Lord deemed necessary ; organizing a church, ordaining priesthoods, and things pertaining to the notification of the Gentiles generally, and to fill up the volume of revelation and prophecy, sufficiently so as to enable all honest seekers after truth to obtain the knowledge necessary for their salvation. But he was not called to do the work; the Lord prepared another man for that purpose, and gave power to Joseph Smith and Oliver Cowdery to bring that priesthood to light; and this they did in a manner beyond the possibility of a successful contradiction, that all might see and understand; and if they did not, it was their sin and not their excuse. It was said to the church through Joseph Smith, that if he were taken, he should have power only to appoint another in his stead. (Section 14th, paragraph 2d, Book of Doctrine and Covenants.) Now to say that if a man should be equal to himself in holding the keys of the kingdom, and also the keys of the school of the prophets, was not making that appointment, we should like to know what would do or could do it. Put in connection with this his carrying to the Lamanites the gospel of their salvation, and their receiving it at his hand; and that he should turn to the Jews, and then the arm of the Lord should be revealed in power; and then all should hear the gospel in their own tongue; that through him the Lord's people should be pure as Christ was; and that the blind should see, the lame should walk, the deaf should hear, and devils should be cast out, and the heavens should shake for his good. All this said concerning one man, to the exclusion of all others. From all these facts, let any and all judge whether Joseph Smith did or did not appoint a man to lead Zion.

Add to these that the Lord said that he should be blessed, and do great things; for he had been sent forth to prepare the way before Christ and Elijah that should come. Taking the foregoing promises and prophecies, and say, Will they amount to an appointment? If they do all controversy ends?

To place this matter in all its force, we will here transcribe the 2d paragraph of the 14th section of the Book of Doctrine and Covenants, which says: "But verily, verily, I say unto you, that none shall be appointed unto this gift, except it shall be through him; for, if it be taken from him, he shall not have power, except to appoint another in his stead; and this shall be a law unto you, that you receive not the teachings of any that shall come before you as revelations or commandments: and this I give unto you, that you may not be deceived, that you may know that they are not of me. For, verily, I say unto you, that he that is ordained of me, shall come in at the gate, and be ordained, as I have told you before, *to teach those revelations* which you have received, and shall receive through him whom I have appointed."

It is of importance, in understanding the quotation above, that the person that was to follow after Joseph Smith was taken, was to be appointed and ordained to that office, and he was to be a *teacher of the revelations* which the church had received, and should hereafter receive. What farther evidence need we that the church was to be directed by those revelations? or else why should there be one ordained to teach them? How manifest the duty of returning to the Book of Mormon and the former commandments by the children of Zion, seeing the Lord was to ordain a man to *teach* them after Joseph Smith was gone. And who could that man be but the one, concerning whom he said he would make him mighty to expound all Scriptures, that he might know the certainty of all things pertaining to the kingdom of heaven on the earth. We certainly think that such testimonies as these could not fail to convince any rational mind.

The subject, when taken in all its departments, assumes a most impressive character. It wants but little reflection to see, that any and all who take upon themselves the authority of teaching and ruling in the house of God, unless they have received it lawfully, must find themselves in an unenviable position, when they do as the Lord has required of them, to turn "to the Book of Mormon and former commandments," and find themselves, as they will find themselves, operating in the face of, and in the defiance of, all the prophecies and promises, made in any or all the books of revelation ever given to man.

Is the Lord a jealous God? Has he a sacred regard for his word? Shall that which has gone out of his mouth never return to him empty? If so, what will be the fate of those who put it at defiance, and rise up against his entire revealed will which he has caused to be written, and yet say they know God, and are his servants? We have men doing so now. The Lord has caused his policy to be plainly set forth in his revelations, with a positive requirement that we should turn to it, or else forever remain under condemnation. Will those who have set themselves in opposition to the whole scheme of heaven succeed? Should they do so, they will foil and floor the Almighty, and undeify him in the world; for it is by foreshadowing his policy by the prophets whom he raises up to make his purposes known, and then carrying out the scheme of things thus pre-declared, that he establishes and sustains his character amongst men. This policy, he says, he has pursued from the beginning, and through his entire dealings with the world; and as his course is one eternal round, he will continue to do it.

To us he raised up a prophet, as he did to others. This prophet has, in language not to be mistaken, revealed to us the Lord's purposes concerning his priesthood, and the work he has to do, telling us that by that man—calling him by name—he would convert the Lamanites, gather the house of Israel, save Zion, and prepare the way for his coming. But Brigham Young and young Joseph Smith raise themselves up before Jehovah, and say, "You will do no such thing; for I, Brigham, will do that." "No," says young Smith, "neither your chosen servant nor Brigham shall do it, but I, 'by my great name,' will do it."

The contest then is fairly opened, and the Lord is put to the test, either to be foiled, in his revealed purpose, by these men, and be undeified in the world, or else he must hew them down and cast them into the fire; from whence there is no return. From this alternative there is no escape. Either the Almighty must be dethroned on the earth, or else these men must, with all their supporters, perish forever; for they have placed themselves in direct antagonism to the Almighty. Is it a matter of surprise that the Lord should have said that they were blasphemers, and those who followed them rebellious, and as such cut them off from the land of Zion, and sent them away?

Such is the relation which persons acting as they do sustain to their Maker. To all such we say, in the language of Isaiah, 45th chapter, 9th verse, "Woe unto him that striveth with his Maker. Let the potsherds strive with the potsherds of the earth."

This question resolves itself into the following facts. Was Joseph Smith inspired of the Lord to translate the Book of Mormon? and did the Holy Ghost indite the Book of Doctrine and Covenants? If so, there can be no question about whom the Lord has chosen to be his messenger, to recover the house of Joseph, and restore the tribes of Jacob. As the Lord is a God of truth, he will act according to what he has caused to be written, and all those who are acting in opposition, will by and by open their eyes in hell, being in torment, and of this there can be no doubt. Or, on the other hand, was Joseph Smith the most scandalous and heaven-daring wretch that ever lived, not even Judas Iscariot excepted? One or the other of these is true. If the first, the Lord will vindicate himself. If the latter, our religion is false as Satan, and corrupt as the haunts of perdition. Judge ye which of these positions you will take. If the Lord be God, follow him; but if Brigham Young and Joseph Smith be gods, follow them; for the Lord and they are at as direct opposites as it is possible for them to be.

Taking the place the Lord has assigned to prophecy in his work, and it enables the seeker after truth to judge of the works of men, whether they are of God or not. The Lord always abides by his word. When he causes prophecies to be delivered, his course is to bring to pass that which he has previously made known. If a man is doing the will of God, he is fulfilling prophecy. The course he pursues can be found in the books of revelation; but if he is not doing the will of God, he is acting not in accordance with the revealed will of heaven, but doing that which is in opposition to it, and tends to invalidate what the Lord has declared.

He tells us that his course "is one eternal round," and the books show us that Satan's course is one continued round also. His way of attack is always the same,—to invalidate and falsify what the Lord has said. He thus began his operations in the garden of Eden, and brought death into the world. He got our first parents to believe that the Lord had not told the truth; they acted under that belief, and thereby gave the Devil the rule of the world. Thus he began by falsifying the prophecy the Lord had delivered. Having succeeded in his first attempt, he has pursued the same course ever since. The Lord knowing this lays his commands on all those who put themselves under his guidance, to read and study his *word*, and to abide by his *word*, to make this the rule of their action, because Satan overthrew the world at the commencement, because his word had ceased to be the rule of their action.

The entire effort of the Devil since the beginning, has been to falsify the word of the Lord, and to get men to act in opposition to it; he always knows, if he can succeed in that, he has them in his power. It matters nothing to him how religious they are, if their religion is not in obedience to the revealed will of heaven. Those who, among us, obey the voice of the Lord, and turn to the Book of Mormon and the former commandments, see that Satan, true to his instincts, has attacked us as he has done all others before us. What is or was ever said about Brigham Young's ever ruling the church of God? nothing; or what was about Strang's doing it? nothing; or about Bencemy's doing it? nothing; or about young Joseph Smith's doing it? nothing; but about another man's doing it? half the prophecies and promises in the books are devoted to the purpose of making all know it: that he was the chosen of God to the exclusion of all others. What are these men then doing? *falsifying the word of God*, and nothing else: the very work that the Devil wants them to do, in order that he may get possession of both them and the world.

It is almost universally the case, that those who place themselves in such a relation to the Deity, mark some man as a victim, against whom they lavish their vituperation with unmitigated viciousness: too ignorant to see that it is the Almighty himself against whom they are levelling their shafts. It is his word that they are falsifying, and not man's. Take Brigham Young, for example. He professes to be acting under the power of a priesthood, obtained from and through Joseph Smith, while he uses it for the purpose of falsifying the burden of all the prophecies and promises written by Joseph Smith; in fact, his whole course and all those who are with him, is to falsify what Smith caused to be written, and has left behind him. Could inconsistency reach a higher degree of perfection than this? Be sure they have tried to make a scapegoat of Sidney Rigdon, and corruption itself could not have gone to greater lengths in vilification than they have; but all such attempts are only worthy of their authors. Sidney Rigdon did not write the revelations in the Book of Mormon and the

Book of Doctrine and Covenants, but the Spirit of the Lord through Joseph Smith; and after all their vilification and slander, to-day they read as they always did. It was the Lord, through Joseph Smith, who chose him, called, ordained and qualified him for his great calling, and all their railings are against the Lord himself; and this they will find out, in that day, when the olive-trees are broken down, the people affrighted and fled, and their works destroyed.

There are two organizations now in existence, both of which are operating to thwart the purposes of Heaven, to make his prophecies and promises which he has caused to be written, false, and by doing so, undeify him in the world, and give Satan power in the world, and full sway over the whole empire of man: one led by Brigham Young, and the other by Joseph Smith the younger. The one led by Smith is the most forbidding of the two, because it was his own father that was revelator, and it is the prophecies and promises which came through him, that the son is trying to falsify. If it were possible for him to do so, he would sink his father's memory into everlasting shame, and would undeify the Lord in the world, and give Satan full dominion on the earth; but the decree of Jehovah has already gone forth that he will fail, be cut off and cast into the fire. But here we will leave them to their fate, after directing the attention of the reader to the words of Nephi, written for this very case. They are found in the 2d Book of Nephi, chapter 15th, and read thus: "Behold, there are many that harden their hearts against the Holy Spirit, that it hath no place in them. Wherefore, they cast away many things which are written, and esteem them as things of nought."

This covers the whole ground. Men deny the words of the Lord only when they are without the Spirit. Such, then, are the people of the above-mentioned organizations. They have lost the Spirit, and Satan leads them captive at his will. That they deny the things that are written, all know who read the books at all. But we pass to the eighth section.

SECTION VIII.

Let us inquire, at the hand of the books, what they say about the time when the work for fulfilling the covenant to the house of Israel will commence. In the first Book of Nephi and third chapter, the prophet says: "And it came to pass, that I beheld that the wrath of God was poured out upon the great and abominable church, insomuch that there were wars and rumors of wars among all nations and kindreds of the earth; and as there began to be wars and rumors of wars among all the nations which belonged to the mother of abominations, the angel spake unto me, saying, Behold, the wrath of God is upon the mother of harlots; and behold thou seest all these things; and when the day cometh that the wrath of God is poured out upon the mother of harlots, which is the great and abominable church of all the earth, whose foundation is the Devil, then at that day the work of the Father shall commence in *preparing* the way for the fulfilling of his covenants, which he hath made to his people who are of the house of Israel."

The language of the prophet, in this case, is very explicit, and there is no need of mistake. We are told positively, the work of the Father in beginning *to prepare* the way to fulfil the covenant to the house of Israel, is to take place after the wars and rumors of wars shall be among all the nations that belong to the great and abominable church. These sayings could not apply to any thing which has yet taken place since the coming forth of the Book of Mormon. When that came forth, there was a time of peace throughout all the civilized world, and continued so for many years afterwards; and it is but just now, as it were, that the nations of the earth have assumed and are assuming the character here given to them.

All that has taken place among that people who believed the Book of Mormon, has never reached even the work of *beginning to prepare* to fulfil the covenant, let alone to fulfil the covenant.

This *beginning to prepare* the way for fulfilling the covenant is, according to the books, the dawning of the great and marvellous work, so much spoken of in the Books of Mormon and Doctrine and Covenants; so says the Book of Mormon, 2d Nephi, chapter 11th. "The Lord will set his hand again the second time to restore his people from their lost and fallen state. Wherefore, he will proceed to do a marvellous work and a wonder among the children of men." Solemn the thought, and sublime the contemplation, that after the lapse of over thirty years from the time the annunciation was first made, the mere shadow of the work should begin to throw itself before; but such is the fact.

A retrospect, going far back, only increases the solemnity of the field of contemplation, in consequence of the established usages of heaven, as made known through the revealed will of the Deity, and fills the mind with awe. When the Lord rejected the house of Eli, he cut it off; when he rejected that of Saul, he cut that off also; and when John the Baptist stepped aside from the duty assigned him, and took it upon himself to meddle with the affairs of the political rulers, Christ let him be cut off; and when we come nearer to our own times, when the Smith family was rejected of God, he cut them off. Strang has also been cut off for setting his feet in places where the Lord had not authorized him to do it; and we have the Lord's word for it that Brigham Young and those with him will be cut off. From all these examples, surely the people whom the Lord has notified that through them he is going to proceed to begin the work of *preparing* to fulfil the covenant made to the house of Israel, will find it important to study well the word of the Lord, and walk as he has directed.

Now, for the sum of the whole matter. If Sidney Rigdon does not convert the Lamanites, restore the tribes of Jacob, bring salvation to Zion, and purify the saints, so they can see the face of the Lord; and if, under his administration, the blind do not see, the lame walk, the dumb speak, the heavens shake, and the arm of the Lord be revealed in power, in convincing the nations: then, indeed, the books of revelation we have are a tissue of falsehoods, and all our religion vain; Joseph Smith, a base falsifier, an imp of Satan, instead of a prophet of the living God.

APPENDIX.

In connection with the Appeal, we feel it our privilege to add our testimony. While engaged in the practice of our profession, as a physician, which is the profession for which we were educated, and to which we have devoted all our energies from our youth to the present time, we were startled and overwhelmed by the visions of heaven which were manifested to us; the visions of heaven we say, because no power except that of the Most High could ever have surrounded us with them. We were lost in wonder and astonishment. The Spirit of the Lord, which accompanied the divine manifestation, directed us to Mr. Newton, one of the authors of the preceding Appeal, for instruction, and for administration and induction into the kingdom of heaven. Mr. Newton had never spoken to us on the subject, nor we to him; but so terrible was the divine manifestation, that we visited him and sought counsel at his hand; and the result was, that we were administered to by him, according to the laws and ordinances of the kingdom of heaven. Of this we could have no doubt; for we were certain that the Judge of all the earth would not deceive us, and as he sent us to Mr. Newton himself, no deception could exist in the case, as the whole matter was between the great God and ourselves. Consequently we know that the authors of the preceding Appeal are men of God, and are such as the Lord acknowledges, and whose priesthood he approves, and to whose administration, in his name, he gives the seal of the Holy Spirit.

We, therefore, do know that the persons who have sent forth the Appeal, dedicated to the Latter-Day Saints, are the people of God.

JOSEPH W. ROWE, M.D.

www.ingramcontent.com/pod-product-compliance
Lightning Source LLC
Chambersburg PA
CBHW022149090426
42742CB00010B/1444